Where Is Jesus?

Where Is Jesus?

Copyright © 1997 by Abingdon Press

This book is printed on recycled, acid-free elemental-chlorine-free paper.

ISBN 0-687-45869-2

This story is based on Luke 2:41-52.

97 98 99 00 01 02 03 04 05 06—10 9 8 7 6 5 4 3 2 1
Printed in Hong Kong

Where Is Jesus?

Sharilyn S. Adair and Sheila K. Hewitt
Illustrated by Bob Jones

Abingdon Press

"Jesus, here is a loaf of bread for our lunch," says Mary. "Mmm, good. I like your bread, Mother," says Jesus. "I'll put it on the donkey." Jesus is helping his father, Joseph, pack the donkey for a trip to Jerusalem.

"Hee-haw," says the donkey.

Many people are traveling to Jerusalem. Some of them ride donkeys. Some walk beside their donkeys. Sometimes Jesus walks with his parents, but sometimes he walks with his cousins.

Finally the travelers arrive in Jerusalem. Joseph stops at a colorful booth to buy some fruit. "Look!" says Jesus. "See how many people are here. Everyone is happy to be celebrating the Passover."

Jesus and his family go to the Temple. "This is the largest building I have ever seen," says Jesus.

Jesus loves the Temple.
He likes to sit and listen
to the teachers there.

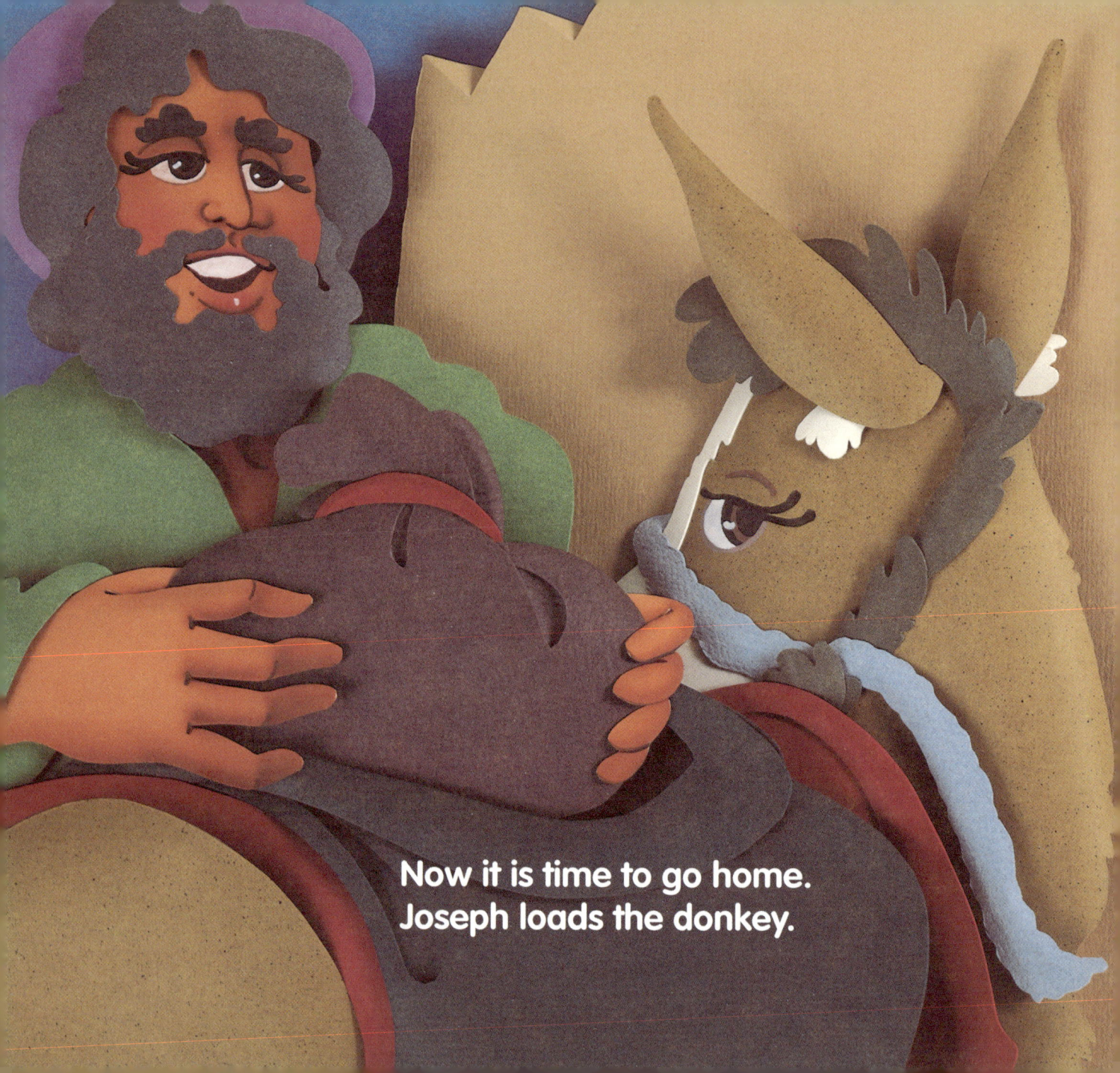

Now it is time to go home.
Joseph loads the donkey.

But Jesus is still talking with the teachers.

The travelers walk all day. When night comes, they stop.
They put up their tents and build a cooking fire.

"Where is Jesus?" asks Mary. "Is he with you, Joseph?"
"No, Jesus is not with me," says Joseph."
They look for Jesus.

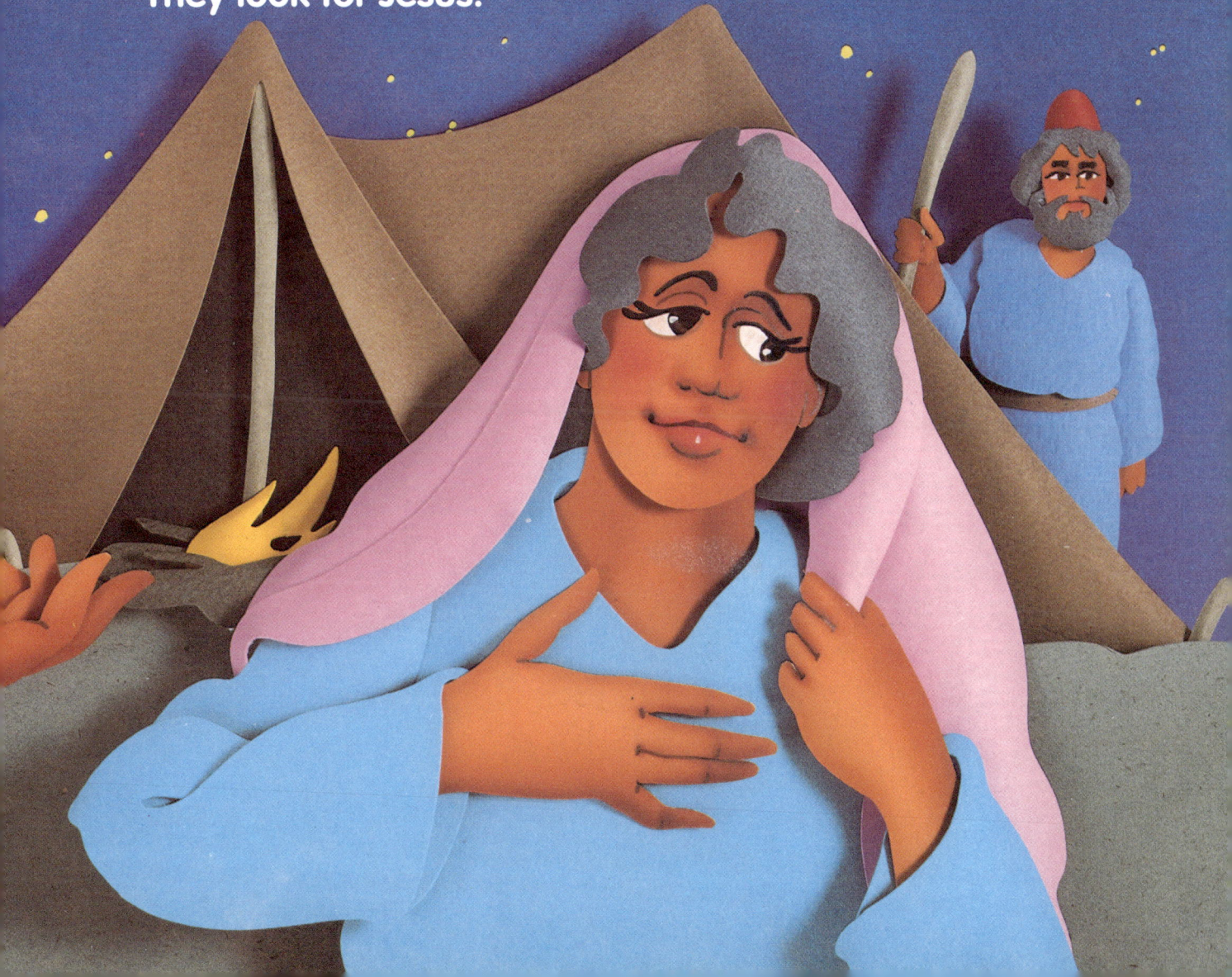

"Is that Jesus standing behind our neighbor Aaron?" asks Mary.

"No, I am Simon," says the boy.

"Is Jesus behind that bush?" asks Joseph. But Jesus is not behind the bush.

Mary says, "Jesus is not here, Joseph. We must go back to Jerusalem to find him."

"Look!" says Joseph. "Is Jesus in the window of that house?" But Jesus is not in the window of the house.

"Jesus is behind that jar!" says Joseph. But Jesus is not behind the jar.

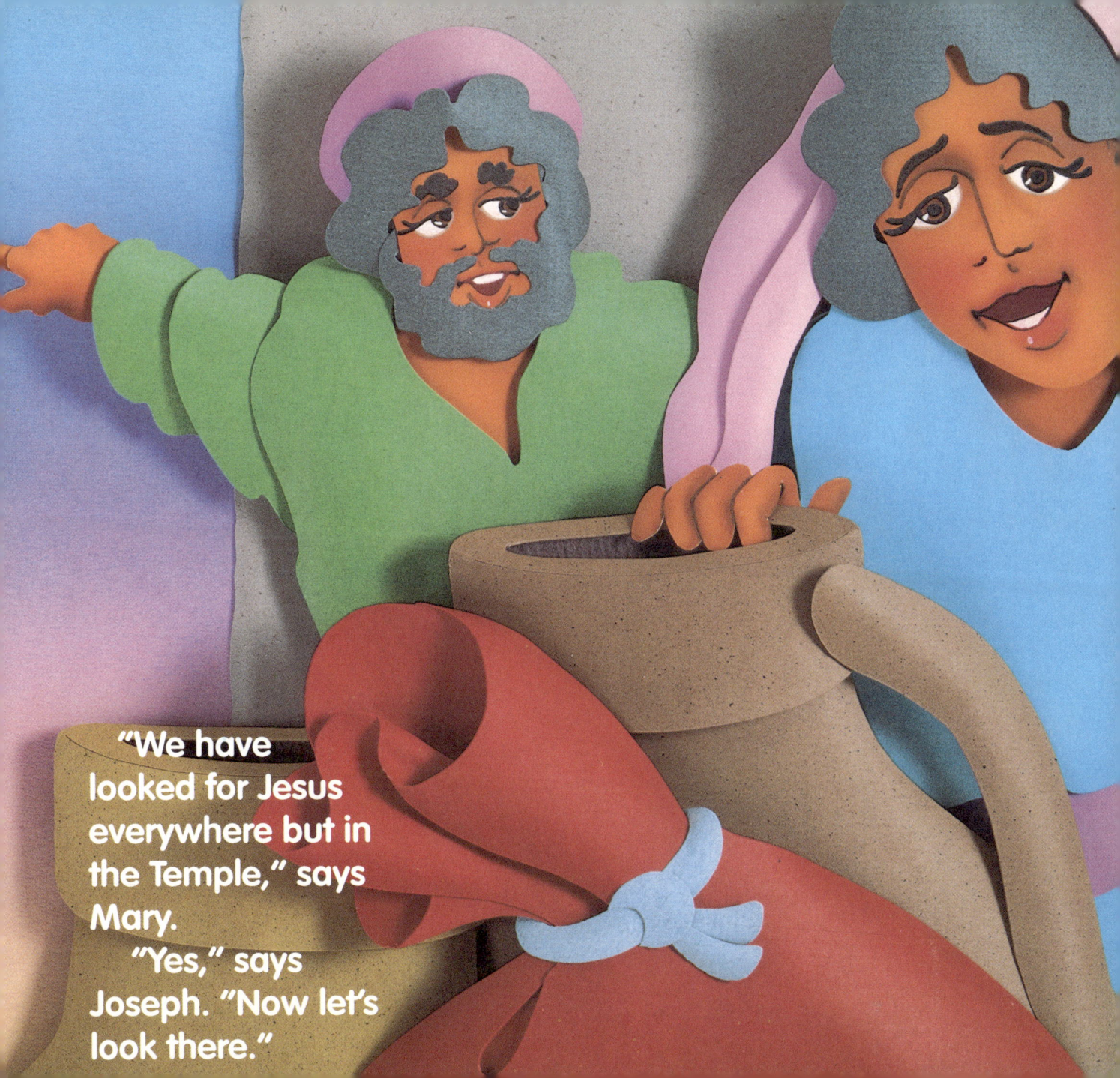

"We have looked for Jesus everywhere but in the Temple," says Mary.

"Yes," says Joseph. "Now let's look there."

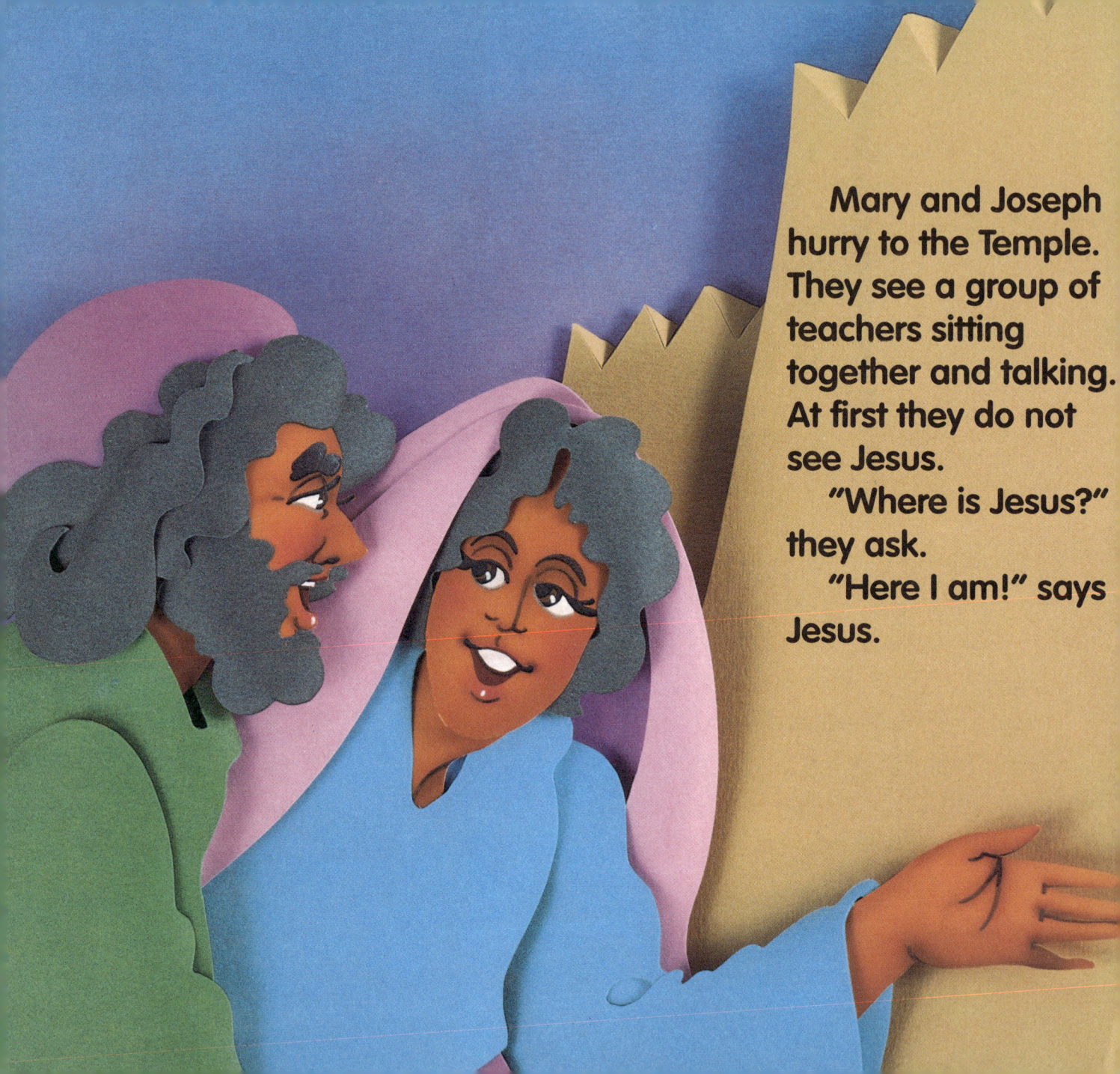

Mary and Joseph
hurry to the Temple.
They see a group of
teachers sitting
together and talking.
At first they do not
see Jesus.

"Where is Jesus?"
they ask.

"Here I am!" says
Jesus.

"Jesus, we were worried about you. We thought you were lost," says Mary.

"I wasn't lost, Mother," says Jesus. "I have been right here in the Temple all the time. I have been learning about God."

"Come along, Son, it's time to go home now," says Joseph. Jesus goes home with his parents.

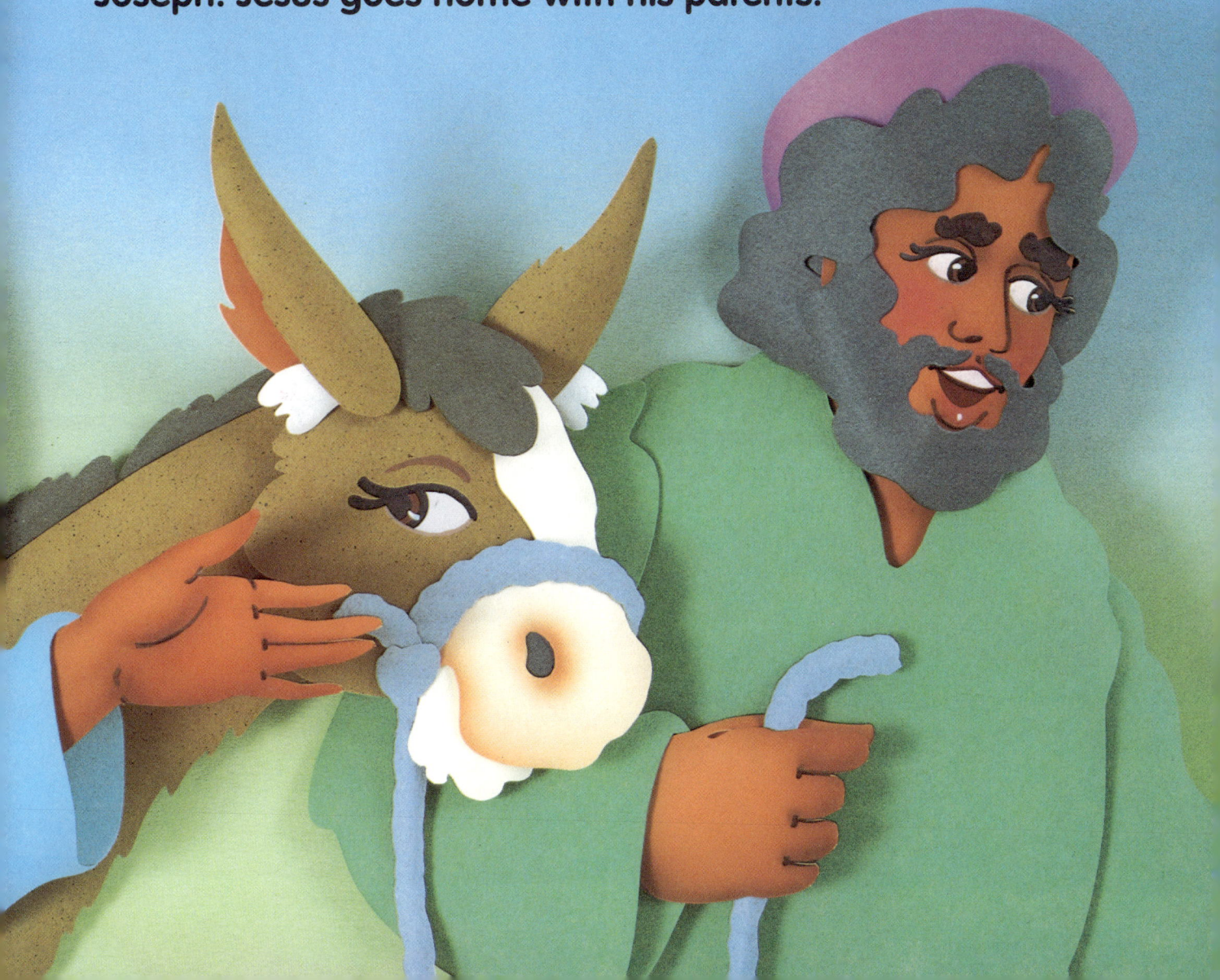

Jesus obeys his parents and grows tall and strong. Everyone likes him, and God likes him too.